PUFFIN BOOKS

THE STARS AND PLANETS
A BEGINNER'S GUIDE TO SPACE

Have you ever wondered what it would be like to land on Jupiter, why some stars look brighter than others, or what would happen if the Sun stopped shining?

From detailed fact files about the planets to instructions for making a simple shadow-clock, this book is full of information for first-time star-gazers. Whether you want to fly to the Moon or prefer to keep your feet on the ground and explore the sky from Earth, this is a marvellous introduction to the exciting and mysterious world of space.

Brian Jones is the author of many books and articles on space exploration and astronomy for both adults and children. He also runs a picture library, supplying material on space for use in books, magazines and journals. He lives in Bradford, Yorkshire.

Brian Jones

The Stars and Planets

A Beginner's Guide to Space

Illustrated by
Frank James

PUFFIN BOOKS

PUFFIN BOOKS

Published by the Penguin Group
Penguin Books Ltd, 27 Wrights Lane, London W8 5TZ, England
Penguin Books USA Inc., 375 Hudson Street, New York, New York 10014, USA
Penguin Books Australia Ltd, Ringwood, Victoria, Australia
Penguin Books Canada Ltd, 10 Alcorn Avenue, Toronto, Ontario, Canada M4V 3B2
Penguin Books (NZ) Ltd, 182–190 Wairau Road, Auckland 10, New Zealand

Penguin Books Ltd, Registered Offices: Harmondsworth, Middlesex, England

Published in Puffin Books 1993
1 3 5 7 9 10 8 6 4 2

Text copyright © Brian Jones, 1993
Illustrations copyright © Frank James, 1993
All rights reserved

The moral right of the author has been asserted

Typeset by Datix International Limited, Bungay, Suffolk
Filmset in Lasercomp Times
Printed in England by Clays Ltd, St Ives plc

Contents

Chapter 1

Is There Life in Outer Space?

Have you ever seen a flying saucer? If not, perhaps you wish you had. Everyone is fascinated by outer space and the idea of worlds beyond our own. Scientists who are especially interested in space and who try to find out more about the stars and planets are called astronomers. It is because of astronomers that we already know so much about space, but there is still plenty more that we don't know, which is why astronomy is so exciting: new discoveries are being made all the time!

But could those flying saucers, or UFOs

(Unidentified Flying Objects), *really* be spaceships carrying beings from other planets and galaxies (star systems)? Some people believe they are, but it is very unlikely that we are being visited by aliens.

The Earth is one of nine planets going round, or orbiting, the Sun. Together they are known as a solar system. None of the other planets in our solar system is able to support life. Mercury and Venus are both

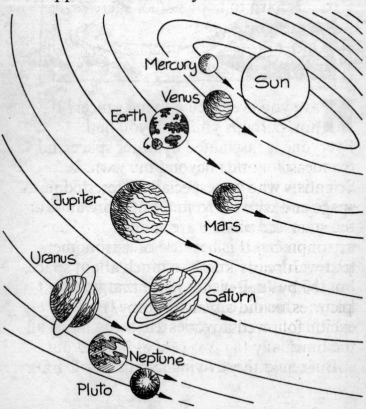

too hot, Pluto is too cold, and Jupiter, Saturn, Uranus and Neptune are too gassy – they do not have solid surfaces.

However, there may be other groups of planets elsewhere in the Universe. Our galaxy contains thousands of millions of stars. Many of these stars are very much like the Sun, and some may have planets going around them. Astronomers think they have found a number of planets around other stars. But the stars are so far away that it is hard to tell whether there really *are* planets orbiting them.

If other groups of planets *do* exist, will there be life on them?

MAKING CONTACT

Some astronomers have tried to make contact with aliens. This has been done in a number of ways. In March 1972, American scientists launched an unmanned rocket (a space probe), *Pioneer 10*, to explore the planet Jupiter. Nearly two years later it passed by Jupiter and sent back good pictures, as did a second probe, *Pioneer 11*, which followed a year later.

Eventually the two probes headed out into deep space, from where they will never

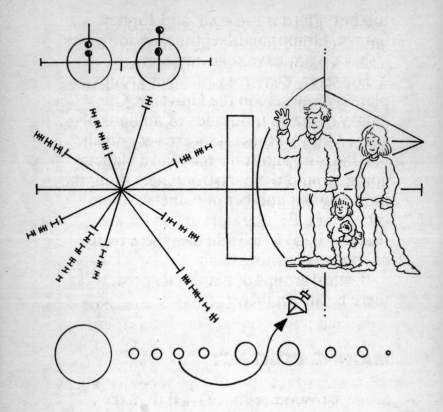

return. But fastened to each one is a special plaque. On this plaque are pictures and other information showing where the probes come from and what human beings look like. If either spacecraft is picked up by aliens, they will be able to tell where humans live.

In 1977, the *Pioneer* probes were followed by two more, *Voyager 1* and *Voyager 2*. Both spacecraft explored Jupiter and

Saturn, and *Voyager 2* went on to Uranus and Neptune. The *Voyager* probes each carry a record of many different sounds from planet Earth. These include greetings in lots of different languages, animal sounds and music. There is also a stylus to play the record and instructions telling any aliens who find it how to do so. The chances of aliens finding any of these probes are very tiny, but it may happen.

As well as sending things out into space, astronomers are listening in to the Universe to see if they can pick up any radio signals sent out by other intelligent beings. No messages have been detected so far, but they will keep on trying!

Scientists have also beamed radio messages to the stars in the hope that aliens may pick them up. The problem here is that the stars are so far away that the radio messages will take many years to get there. Even then there may be nobody listening!

One message which was sent in 1974 is being transmitted to the Great Globular Cluster of stars. This huge cluster contains many thousands of stars. Perhaps one of them has a planet orbiting it on which there is life! If so, and if they hear our greeting, they may send a message back. However, the Great Globular Cluster is so far away that we would not receive their message for about another 50,000 years!

WHAT WILL ALIENS LOOK LIKE?

If we ever did find beings elsewhere in the Universe, what would they look like? They may not be like humans at all. What they look like will depend on the conditions in which they live. Creatures on Earth have grown to suit their surroundings. A good example are polar bears, which have developed thick fur to protect them against the cold Arctic weather.

It would probably be the same in other worlds. Planets with thin air may have life forms with huge lungs to take in enough air to allow them to breathe. Planets with suns which are not very bright may be home to beings with large eyes which would allow them to see in the dark. Planets orbiting cool stars may have creatures with thick fur-covered skins to protect them against the cold.

One thing is for certain: until we actually make contact with alien civilizations we will not know what they look like. Until then, we can only imagine . . .

So let's have a look at what we *do* know.

Chapter 2

The View from Planet Earth

Morning   Noon   Evening

Have you noticed how the Sun appears to move across the sky? It rises in the east in the morning. Then it crosses the sky to set (go down) in the west in the evening. The stars seem to move in the same way. But the Sun and stars are not really moving at all. They appear to move only because the Earth is spinning round, or rotating. This rotation of the Earth causes night and day.

When the Sun rises in the morning we have day and when it sets we have night. The Sun shines on only one half of the Earth at a time. It is day on the half

which is facing the Sun and night on the
other half. When it is daytime in Britain,
people in Australia are asleep in bed! We
can't see the stars during the daytime. This
is because the light from the Sun blots them
out.

The Earth is spinning on its axis, rather
like a huge spinning-top and it takes just
under twenty-four hours to make one
complete turn. The Earth's axis is an
imaginary line passing through the Earth
from north to south. Its ends are called the
North and South Poles. It is like the handle
of the spinning-top. The stars above the
North and South Poles appear to stay still

in the sky. All the other stars appear to go around them. If you watch the Pole-star carefully, it will seem to stay in the same position all night. But all the other stars will slowly wheel around it.

You can see how day and night happen for yourself. Take a torch and a beach-ball. Pretend the torch is the Sun and the ball is the Earth. Now, in a darkened room, shine the torch on to the ball. You will see that only half the ball is lit up. Put a mark on

the ball with a felt pen. Spin the ball and you will see that the mark moves around. It will spend half the time in "daylight" and half in "night". This experiment looks even better if you use a globe of the Earth instead of the beach-ball!

As you get to know the stars in the sky, you will see that different stars appear at different seasons. The group of stars, or constellation, called Orion can be seen in

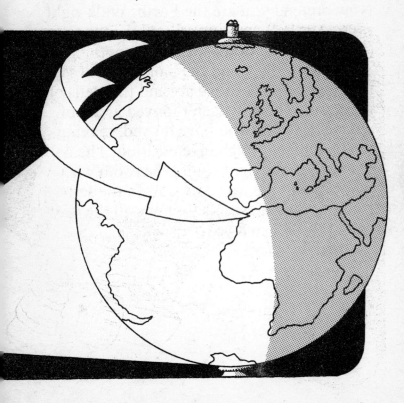

winter but has disappeared by the time summer comes. This is because the Earth is moving around the Sun. We call its path around the Sun an orbit. The Earth takes just over 365 days to travel once around the Sun. We call this length of time a year.

As the Earth moves along its orbit, the Sun appears to move through the sky. You can do an experiment to see why this happens. Put a ball on a chair in the middle of a room. Imagine the ball is the Sun. Now pretend you are the Earth. Walk right round the ball, looking at it all the time. (Be careful you don't walk into anything!)

As you walk round the ball, you will see that it appears to move around the walls of the room. The ball hasn't moved at all, of course. It is *you* who have moved, making the ball appear to change position. The ball seems to move right round the room when you walk all the way round it. In the same fashion, the Sun seems to move all the way round the sky in a year.

Chapter 3
The Nearest Star

The Sun is a star. Like all the other stars in the sky, the Sun is a very hot ball of gas. It is also very bright. The Sun appears much brighter than the other stars because it is so much closer to us. If the Sun were as far away as the other stars, it would seem quite faint.

We did not always know that the Sun was a star. Long ago, people from different countries told stories to explain what they thought the Sun was. One of these came from the Australian Aboriginals, who said that the Sun was a huge bonfire in the sky. This bonfire was lit every morning by the gods of the sky to light up the Earth during the daytime.

The Sun has no flames and does not burn like a fire. If it did, it would burn up and go out very quickly. So how does the Sun make its energy and keep shining? Deep at the Sun's centre, one kind of gas is being changed into another. As this happens, some of the original gas escapes to the surface. From here it leaves the Sun as light and heat, so making the Sun shine.

The Sun is so bright that you would damage your eyes if you looked directly at it. You must *never* look at the Sun through binoculars or a telescope; otherwise you could be blinded.

There is only one really safe way to look at the Sun. A telescope can be pointed at it so that a picture of the Sun is thrown on to a piece of white card. The telescope is used in much the same way as a magnifying glass is used to burn something. The magnifying glass makes a small, hot spot of light on the thing you are trying to burn. This bright spot is a tiny picture of the Sun. This picture is called an image. The telescope does the same thing, but the image it gives is much bigger and clearer.

You must *never* look through the telescope when you are lining it up with the Sun. Instead, just point it in roughly the right direction and move it about until you

get an image of the Sun on your piece of card. Even if it takes a long time to line the telescope up properly, be patient. It is better to do this than risk damaging your eyes.

When you look at the Sun this way, you may see some dark patches on its surface. These are sunspots, and they come in many different sizes. Some sunspots have been so large that they were visible without a telescope or binoculars!

Sunspots appear dark only because they

are cooler than the surrounding surface. If you could see a sunspot away from the glare of the Sun, it would appear quite bright. If you look at the Sun twice, a few days apart, you may see that the sunspot seems to change its position on the Sun's surface. This is because the Sun is spinning and carrying the sunspot around with it.

There are lots of different things happening on the Sun. For example, huge jets and streamers of very hot gas sometimes leap up from its surface at very high speeds. These are called prominences. Prominences have many different shapes and no two are ever exactly alike. Unfortunately, you will be able to see prominences only with quite a large telescope.

MAKING A SHADOW-CLOCK

Because the Earth spins on its axis, the Sun appears to move across the sky. When the Sun is shining, it casts shadows. The shadow you know best is your own. You can see how the Sun moves by looking at your shadow at different times of the day.

On a sunny day, mark a spot on the ground and stand there. Get a friend to draw with chalk the outline of your

shadow. Stand in the same spot, facing the same direction, a couple of hours later. Ask your friend to draw your shadow again. You will see that its position has changed. This is because the position of the Sun in the sky is different.

To make a shadow-clock, you will need a flat piece of wood and a long nail. Get an adult to hammer the nail into the piece of wood. Now stand the wood so that the nail is upright and the wood will be in sunlight all day.

You will see that the nail casts a shadow. Mark the position of the shadow in the early morning. Write the time next to the shadow. Now go out every hour and do the same. Remember to keep the wood in the same position all the time.

By late afternoon you will have made a simple shadow-clock. You can use this clock, which we call a sundial, over the next few days to tell the time. To do this, mark its exact position by drawing a chalk outline around it. Put it back in the same place the next day. The shadow of the nail will be lined up with your drawings of its shadow at the same times.

You will notice something odd about the length of the shadow at different times. In the morning and afternoon it will be longer than it is at midday. This is because at midday the Sun is higher in the sky and the shadows it casts are shorter. Also, the Sun is higher in the sky in summer than in winter.

Chapter 4
The Moon

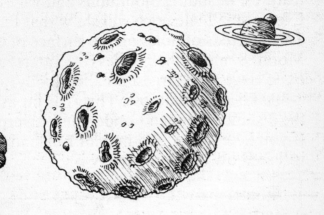

The Moon is our closest neighbour in space, even though it is about 384,400 kilometres away from us! Because it is so close we can examine its surface quite easily. The first thing we notice when we look at the Moon is that its surface is a mixture of light and dark areas. The dark patches are called "maria", which is the Latin word meaning "seas".

A long time ago, before the telescope was invented, astronomers thought that there was water on the Moon and that the dark areas were seas. They gave them names such as Mare Nubium, meaning Sea of Clouds, and Mare Frigoris, meaning Sea of Cold.

We now know that the Moon has no water on it, but the old names are still used.

The bright areas contain lots of different features, including mountains and valleys. Even a small telescope will show that there are hundreds of holes on the surface of the Moon. Some of these holes (or craters) are quite large. The largest is called Bailly, and is 300 kilometres across. This is as far as the distance between London and Liverpool. If you take a look at a map of England you will see how big Bailly really is.

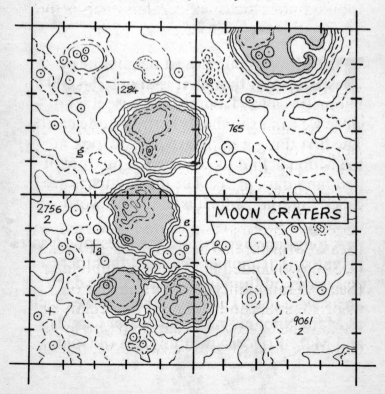

MOON CRATERS

How were the Moon's seas and craters formed? A long time ago, when the Moon was still very young, it was hit by lots of meteorites (lumps of metal or rock). Each time a meteorite hit the Moon it left a crater. Soon the whole of the Moon was covered in craters. Then volcanoes erupted, spilling out molten lava on to the surface of the Moon. This lava filled all the lowland areas, just like water does here on Earth. Many of the craters were buried, leaving a mixture of dried-up lava beds and mountainous areas with craters. This is the surface that we see today.

DRAWING A MAP OF THE MOON

Even without a telescope or binoculars, you can see lots of different features on the Moon. The dark patches – the seas – are easiest to see. There are quite a few large ones, including Oceanus Procellarum (Ocean of Storms) and Mare Humorum (Sea of Moisture). The *Apollo 11* astronauts (see below) landed in Mare Tranquillitatis (Sea of Tranquillity). Craters appear only as bright spots and you need binoculars or a telescope to see their shapes. If you look carefully, you will see the two large, bright craters called Tycho and Copernicus. Tycho is 85 kilometres across and Copernicus is 93 kilometres.

When you are looking at the Moon through binoculars or a telescope, find the line dividing its light and dark parts. This line is called the "terminator". Any features seen here will stand out really well because they cast long shadows across the Moon's surface.

There are a lot of stories about the Moon.

The most famous tells of the man in the Moon: the dark areas are supposed to make a pattern looking like a human face. A story from Germany says that he was put on the Moon as a punishment for stealing cabbages from one of his neighbours.

The Maoris of New Zealand tell a story about a woman in the Moon. This woman was called Rona and she was angry at the Moon. The Moon punished her and tried to pull her up into the sky. She tried to stay on Earth by hanging on to a tree, but the Moon pulled so hard that Rona and the tree came away together!

Take a close look at the Moon without a telescope or binoculars. Can you see either the German thief or Rona clutching the tree? Can you make out any other patterns of your own? Why not try drawing the Moon as a circle on a piece of paper and put in any features that you can see on its surface.

THE PHASES OF THE MOON

If you watch the Moon carefully over a few weeks you will see that it appears to change shape. These different "shapes" are called phases. It doesn't really change shape, of course. It only seems to because it is changing position in the sky as it goes round the Earth.

On the Moon, a "day" is much longer than it is at home. The Earth spins round once in twenty-four hours, so that we have about twelve hours of daylight and twelve hours of night (although this does

change according to the time of year: the
days are longer in the summer than in the
winter). The Moon spins round not in
twenty-four hours, but in just over
twenty-seven days, so that a "day" there
is almost as long as two Earth weeks, and
is followed by a two-week-long "night".

The Moon also takes just over
twenty-seven days to make one
journey round the Earth. This means that
the same side of the Moon is turned
towards us all the time. Try walking round
a chair, keeping your face turned towards
the chair. Anyone sitting on the chair will
never see the back of your neck, and from
Earth we can never see the "back" of the
Moon.

The only reason we see the Moon at all

is because it is lit up by the Sun. Only half
the Moon is lit up at any time. The phase,
or shape, we see depends on how much of
the lit half is facing the Earth.

When the Moon is between the Earth
and the Sun, the dark half is turned towards
us and the Moon is invisible. This is called a
New Moon. As the Moon moves round the
Earth, we see a thin slice of the lit half,
which can be seen in the evening sky shortly
after sunset. As the nights pass and the Moon
continues its journey round the Earth, we
gradually see more of the Moon, until the
whole of the lit half is facing us and we see
a Full Moon. The Moon is now exactly
opposite the Sun in the sky. A Full Moon
rises in the east at the same time as the Sun
sets in the west.

After Full Moon the phases go "backwards" until once again we can see only a thin slice. This time the slice appears in the morning sky, just before sunrise. Finally there is another New Moon. It takes twenty-nine and a half days (about a month) for the Moon to change from New to Full and back to New again.

LANDING ON THE MOON

Men and women have always dreamt of going to the Moon. A long time ago, the ancient Greeks believed that a huge waterspout would be able to lift a sailing-ship up to the Moon! But it was not until the twentieth century that the first people actually walked on the Moon. There was a lot of work to do before that was possible.

The first spacecraft to visit the Moon did not have any people on board, but with the information it sent back to Earth scientists were able to make maps of the Moon and study its surface more closely. This helped them to pick landing-sites and to plan what the astronauts would do when they got there.

American scientists sent ranger probes to

Lunar Orbiter

Lunar Surveyor

crash-land on the Moon, taking
pictures as they fell. Other spacecraft, called
Surveyor probes, made soft landings. They
took lots of photographs, and also carried
out experiments to test the soil on the
Moon, to see whether it would stand the
weight of humans walking there. Both the
Americans and the Russians ran test flights,
sending rockets and astronauts into space,
but they did not land.

Then, in July 1969, Neil Armstrong,
Edwin Aldrin and Michael Collins blasted
off to the Moon in a spacecraft called
Apollo 11. The spacecraft was in two parts:
the Command Module and the Lunar

(Moon) Module. The astronauts travelled in the Command Module. When they got near the Moon, Neil Armstrong and Edwin Aldrin got into the Lunar Module. It separated from the Command Module when they arrived and took them down to the Moon's surface. The Command Module stayed in orbit around the Moon, and Michael Collins remained on board. He never actually landed on the Moon.

Neil Armstrong was the first to leave the Lunar Module and step out on to the Moon. He was followed by Edwin Aldrin a few moments later. They found a bare world. The sky was black, because there was no air to scatter sunlight around or make the sky blue as there is on the Earth. Because there is no air on the Moon the astronauts had to wear special suits and helmets. They also had to carry their own air supply to breathe. There are no clouds, water, winds or weather on the Moon – all things we take for granted here on Earth.

The Moon is much smaller than the Earth and its gravity is a lot less. Gravity is the force which holds us down on Earth and stops us floating away. You feel heavy because the Earth is trying to pull you to its centre. The Moon's pull is much weaker, and the astronauts who landed there found that they weighed only a sixth of what they weighed back on Earth. When they walked they could move only in slow motion. Looking up into the sky they saw their home planet, Earth. It looked much bigger in the sky than the Moon does when seen from here. After a few hours, Neil Armstrong and Edwin Aldrin blasted off from the Moon. They used the top section of the Lunar Module to get back into space. This lifted off from the bottom part, which was used as a launch pad.

Apollo 11 was followed by six more missions to the Moon. The *Apollo 12* mission touched down near one of the Surveyor craft which had landed several years before. They examined the Surveyor craft and brought pieces of it back to Earth.

The *Apollo 13* mission never actually made it to the Moon. On the way out there was an explosion in the spacecraft. The astronauts were in a lot of danger. They had to climb from the Command Module into the Lunar Module, which was still attached to the spacecraft. They used the Lunar Module as a kind of lifeboat. *Apollo 13* flew out to the Moon, passed behind it and then headed back for Earth. The crew did manage to reach home safely, to the relief of millions of people watching on television!

LUNAR MODULE

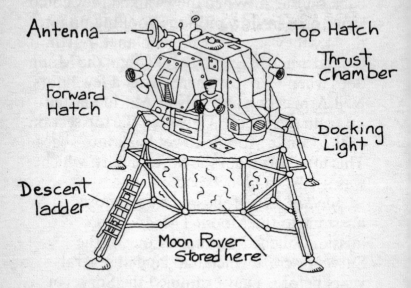

Antenna — Top Hatch

Thrust Chamber

Forward Hatch

Docking Light

Descent ladder

Moon Rover Stored here

During each of the *Apollo* landings, the astronauts carried out experiments. They even left some experiments there to be remotely operated by scientists back on Earth. During the last three *Apollo* missions, the astronauts took a special car, called the Lunar Rover. This allowed them to drive across the Moon and examine much more of it. The Lunar Rovers were left on the Moon and they are still there!

Chapter 5

Hide-and-seek in the Sky

SOLAR ECLIPSES

The Sun is much larger than the Moon. It is also much further away. Because of this, the Sun and Moon *appear* to be nearly the same size when we look up at them from Earth. This is the same as saying your finger is the same size as a lamp-post. If you hold your finger close to your eye, and stand a long way away from the lamp-post, it *will* look the same size, or even bigger!

Sometimes, the Moon passes exactly between the Earth and the Sun. When this

37

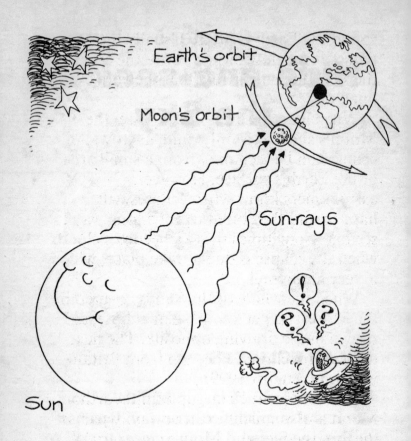

Earth's orbit

Moon's orbit

Sun-rays

Sun

happens the shadow of the Moon falls on the Earth and we get what we call a solar eclipse. If you are standing in the Moon's shadow, the Sun will disappear for a short time.

Solar eclipses happen at New Moon (see page 31), when the dark half of the Moon is facing Earth. So why isn't there an eclipse every month? Because the path of the Moon round the Earth is tilted. Usually the Moon passes just below or just above the Sun in the sky. It is only rarely that they are exactly lined up.

When an eclipse *does* take place, the Moon's shadow is only quite narrow. An eclipse can be seen only from a small area of the Earth's surface. However, astronomers know when eclipses will happen and they often travel a long way to see one. Sometimes the sky becomes cloudy when the eclipse is due to take place, which is very annoying!

When the whole of the Sun is covered by the Moon, we get a *total* solar eclipse, as shown in the drawing opposite. The next total solar eclipse to be seen from Britain will be in August 1999.

Sometimes the lining-up of the Earth, Moon and Sun isn't exact and only part of the Sun is covered. Then we get a *partial* solar eclipse. During partial solar eclipses it looks as if a piece of the Sun is missing from the edge.

Long ago, people were frightened of eclipses, and in China it was thought that a huge dragon was eating the Sun! Chinese astronomers didn't know the real reason for eclipses, but they knew when they were going to happen. When eclipses took place, the people used to go out to bang gongs and make loud noises to frighten the dragon away. Two astronomers once forgot to tell the Chinese Emperor that an eclipse was about to happen and they had their heads chopped off as a punishment.

LUNAR ECLIPSES

As we have seen, the Moon casts a shadow into space. The Earth also casts a shadow and the Moon sometimes moves through it. The only reason that we see the Moon is that its surface is lit up by the Sun. When the Moon passes into the Earth's shadow

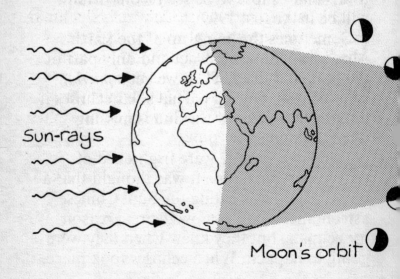

Sun-rays

Moon's orbit

the sunlight is cut off and the Moon gets quite dark. We call this a lunar eclipse. It is only very rarely that the Moon completely disappears. Usually the Moon's surface turns a deep reddish colour.

Lunar eclipses happen at Full Moon, but not every month. Usually the Moon passes either below or above the Earth's shadow.

If all the Moon passes through the Earth's shadow the whole of its surface is plunged into darkness. This is a *total* lunar eclipse. Sometimes, the lining-up isn't exact and only part of the Moon is in shadow. We then get a *partial* lunar eclipse.

When a lunar eclipse takes place, the shadow of the Earth can be seen crossing the Moon. Two thousand years ago, the Greek astronomer Aristotle watched a lunar eclipse. He knew that it was the Earth's shadow making the Moon dark and he noticed that the shadow was curved. The shadow was the same shape during every lunar eclipse and Aristotle worked out that the Earth must be round.

Chapter 6
The Planets

The Earth is a planet which travels round the Sun. There are eight other major planets going round the Sun at the same time, and each has its own path, or orbit. In this chapter, compare what we know about our own planet with the details of the other planets given in the fact files.

For example, if you could draw a line straight through the centre of the Earth, it would measure 12,756 kilometres. We call this its diameter. Pluto, the smallest planet, has a diameter of 2,400 kilometres, only about a fifth of the size of the Earth's. That's about the difference between a marble and a tennis ball.

Earth takes just over 365 days to travel

once around the Sun, and we call this length of time a year. But Mercury takes eighty-eight Earth-days, so a year on Mercury is only eighty-eight Earth-days (about three months) long. But Mercury spins very slowly, so one day on Mercury lasts as long as nearly fifty-nine days on Earth!

The planet Earth is 149.6 million kilometres away from the Sun, but Neptune is 4,496.6 million kilometres from the Sun, which is about thirty times as far! Earth has one satellite: the Moon. A satellite is an object revolving around a planet. So, a fact file for Earth would look like this:

FACT FILE

Diameter: 12,756 km
Distance from the Sun: 149.6 million km
Length of a year: 365.26 Earth-days
Length of a day: 1 Earth-day
Number of satellites: 1

Now let's take a look at the other planets.

MERCURY

FACT FILE

Diameter: 4,880 km
Distance from the Sun: 57.9 million km
Length of a year: 88 Earth-days
Length of a day: 58.65 Earth-days
Number of satellites: 0

Mercury is one of the smallest planets and is always found near the Sun in the sky, which makes it hard to see from Earth. We didn't get our first really good look at Mercury until 1974, when the American space probe *Mariner 10* flew past the planet and sent back pictures of its surface.

Mercury is covered with craters and is a lot like the Moon. It is very hot on Mercury, with temperatures reaching 425°C – over four times the boiling point of water! At night, this drops to minus 180°C, because Mercury has hardly any air to hold in the heat.

VENUS

FACT FILE

Diameter: 12,104 km
Distance from the Sun: 108.2 million km
Length of a year: 224.7 Earth-days
Length of a day: 243 Earth-days
Number of satellites: 0

Venus is the brightest planet, even though it is covered in thick cloud. If you thought Mercury was hot, compare it to Venus. The temperature of Venus is a whopping 480°C, nearly five times the boiling point of water. You would burn to a crisp if you stood on the surface!

Venus is mainly flat, although there are some high areas. The two largest of these high areas are Ishtar Terra and Aphrodite Terra. Ishtar is about as big as Africa. Aphrodite is about the size of Australia.

On top of Ishtar is a huge mountain called Maxwell Montes. This towers 11 kilometres above the surface, over 2 kilometres higher than Mount Everest, the Earth's highest mountain.

MARS

FACT FILE

Diameter: 6,787 km
Distance from the Sun: 227.9 million km
Length of a year: 687 Earth-days
Length of a day: 24.6 Earth-hours
Number of satellites: 2

Mars is often called the Red Planet, because much of it is covered in reddish dust. Dark markings can also be seen. These change in appearance as Martian winds cover and uncover them with dust. Mars also has two polar ice-caps.

The planet has lots of craters, as well as
volcanoes. The largest volcano is called
Olympus Mons and is 25 kilometres high,
over three times as high as Mount Everest!
It measures 600 kilometres across its base,
which makes it big enough to cover the
whole of Ireland. A huge valley called Vallis
Marineris runs across Mars. It is 4,000
kilometres long, and would stretch all the
way across the United States of America.

Because they thought there had been
water on Mars long ago, scientists hoped
there might be life on the planet. Two
American space probes – *Viking 1* and
Viking 2 – landed in 1976. They looked for

signs of life but didn't find any, and most
scientists now think that Mars is a dead
world. The planet has two satellites, or
moons, which travel around it. These are
tiny and irregular in shape. They look a bit
like potatoes! They are probably asteroids
(see below) that wandered too close and
were trapped by the pull of Martian gravity.

THE ASTEROIDS

In between Mars and Jupiter are thousands
of tiny objects we call the asteroids. The
largest is Ceres, which is about 1,000

kilometres in diameter. All the others are much smaller. The only asteroid that can be seen without binoculars or a telescope is Vesta, because it is very bright. Vesta is about half as big as Ceres; the smallest asteroids are probably no bigger than grains of sand.

Sometimes they come quite close to Earth. In January 1991 a tiny asteroid about 10 metres across passed within 170,000 kilometres of us. This is very close indeed, less than half the distance to the Moon. If it had hit the Earth it would have made a big crater and could have caused a lot of damage.

Even the world's largest telescopes show the asteroids only as points of light. We will have to wait until space probes have sent back pictures of asteroids before we know what they really look like.

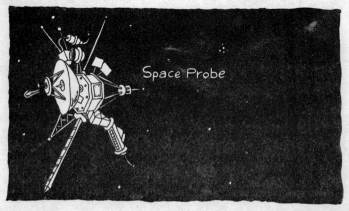

Space Probe

JUPITER

FACT FILE

Diameter: 142,800 km
Distance from the Sun: 778.3 million km
Length of a year: 11.86 Earth-years
Length of a day: 9.84 Earth-hours
Number of satellites: 16

Jupiter is another planet, with a diameter over ten times that of the Earth. It is made of gas. Jupiter is surrounded by light and dark belts of cloud. If you look at Jupiter

through a telescope you will see the two brightest belts. You will also see that Jupiter is quite flat at its poles.

Larger telescopes show a huge oval on the planet. This is the Great Red Spot and is thought to be the top of a huge storm. If you tried to land you would sink for thousands of kilometres. You would eventually hit a rocky centre about the size of Earth. Jupiter has sixteen moons, and you can see the four largest through even quite small telescopes. They are called Io, Ganymede, Europa and Callisto. Space probes have shown that Io has lots of erupting volcanoes on its surfaces. It is very

red and looks a bit like a huge pizza! Ganymede and Callisto have craters scattered all over their surfaces. Europa is covered with frozen water and is very smooth. Some astronomers have even said it looks like a huge snooker ball!

SATURN

FACT FILE

Diameter: 120,000 km
Distance from the Sun: 1,427 million km
Length of a year: 29.46 Earth-years
Length of a day: 10.23 Earth-hours
Number of satellites: 17

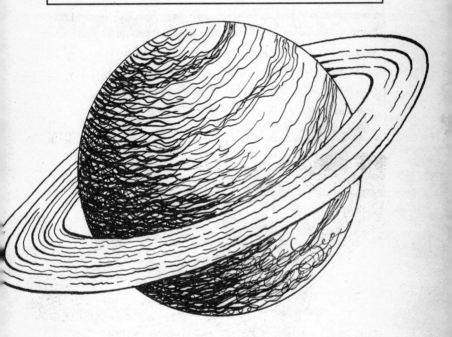

Saturn is another huge gassy planet which also has cloud belts, although these aren't as grand as those of Jupiter. Saturn's ring system makes it the most beautiful of the planets. (Although Jupiter, Uranus and Neptune also have ring systems, these are all very faint and nowhere near as pretty!) The rings are made up of millions of tiny icy particles.

URANUS

FACT FILE

Diameter: 52,400 km
Distance from the Sun: 2,869.6 million km
Length of a year: 84.01 Earth-years
Length of a day: 17.9 Earth-hours
Number of satellites: 15

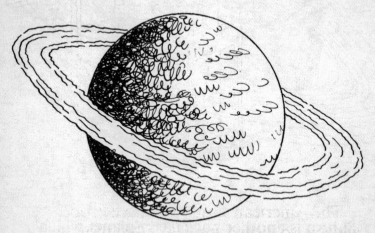

Yet another gassy planet, Uranus is very faint, but you can just see it if the sky is really dark and clear and you know exactly where to look. All the planets we have talked about so far are bright enough to be seen without a telescope and astronomers have known about them for thousands of years. Uranus was discovered by William Herschel in 1781 and was the first planet to be discovered with a telescope.

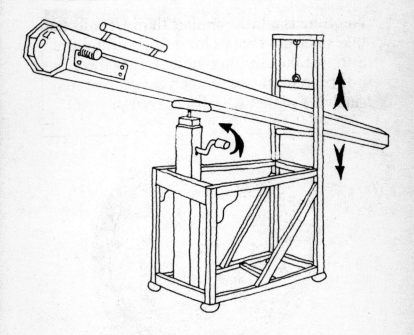

The American *Voyager2* space probe, which also visited Jupiter and Saturn, sent back photographs of Uranus in 1986. The outer surface had few markings or clouds visible.

NEPTUNE

FACT FILE

Diameter: 48,600 km
Distance from the Sun: 4,496.6 million km
Length of a year: 164.8 Earth-years
Length of a day: 19.2 Earth-hours
Number of satellites: 8

Neptune is a little smaller than Uranus and takes about twice as long to go round the Sun. It takes so long, in fact, that there has not been even one whole year on Neptune since the planet was discovered in 1846!

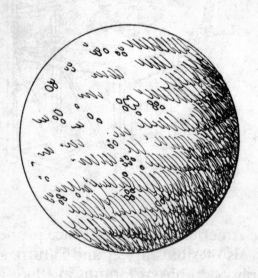

PLUTO

Diameter: 2,400 km
Distance from the Sun: 5,900 million km
Length of a year: 247.7 Earth-years
Length of a day: 6.387 Earth-days
Number of satellites: 1

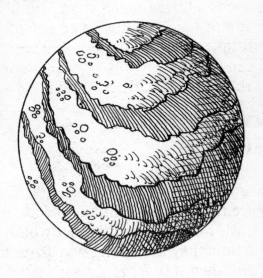

Pluto is a very lonely world, further away
from the Sun than any of the other planets.
It is the smallest of the planets and was
discovered only in 1930.

Chapter 7

Comets, Meteors and Meteorites

COMETS

Comets are not like the planets. They are made up of a mixture of ice, gas and dust, rather like a dirty snowball. Most of the time they are a long way from the Sun and they stay frozen.

However, if a comet gets close to the Sun, the ice in it begins to melt. The gas and dust which were frozen into the comet escape and form a head around the dirty snowball. Some of the material may also be blown away from the head of the comet to form one or more tails.

Not all comets have tails, but some have more than one. Many comets have been seen with two tails. A very bright comet seen 250 years ago actually had six!

Some comets travel around the Sun quickly. The shortest known orbit is that of Encke's Comet. This orbits the Sun once every three and a third years. Other comets take much longer. The most famous comet of all is Halley's Comet. This takes about seventy-six years to go round the Sun. Some comets are known to have such long orbits that astronomers can't tell when they will be coming back!

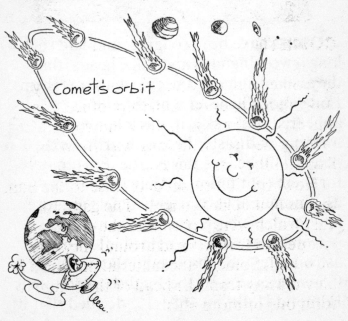

Comet's orbit

Others have been so large, and had such
long, sweeping tails and huge heads, that
they have frightened people who saw them.
Long ago, whenever a bright comet
appeared in the sky, it was taken as a
warning of disaster here on Earth. Some
people still believe this is true. Fortunately
for them (but unfortunately for
astronomers), very bright comets are rare,
and few have been seen this century.

Comets are usually named after the
astronomer who discovered them. Halley's
Comet was seen by the English astronomer
Edmond Halley in 1682. He decided that it

was the same comet that had been seen in 1531 and 1607. He said that it would come back in 1759, and it did! It was named Halley's Comet in his honour, even though he didn't actually discover it. It was last seen in 1986 and will be back again in 2061.

Different comets are seen every year, although not many are really bright. Most appear as fuzzy, glowing patches of light and can be seen only with binoculars or a telescope. Encke's Comet is very faint and you need a large telescope to see it at all, assuming you can find it in the first place! Halley's Comet is much brighter. Because comets orbit the Sun, they are moving through the sky. However, you will need to watch a comet carefully for many hours before you see it change position.

METEORS

As we have seen, dust and gas are pushed away from the head of the comet to form its tail. This dust eventually becomes spread out all along the path of the comet. The bits of dust are very tiny, and can't be seen at all unless they fall to Earth. When this happens the dust burns up as it rubs against the air. This burning-up is caused by friction. The

same sort of thing happens when you rub
your hands together. If you rub hard enough,
friction causes your hands to get quite warm.

When the dust burns up in the air, we see
a streak of light crossing the sky. These
streaks are called meteors. Many people
know them as shooting stars, although they
aren't really stars at all. Meteors move very
quickly and you have to be watching the
sky carefully to see one!

You can see meteors at any time of the
night and at any time of the year. However,
there are times when you will see more
meteors than usual. This is because the
Earth sometimes crosses the orbits of

certain comets. If this happens we may get a meteor shower, when dozens of meteors are seen every hour. The best month to see meteors is August. Other good times are mid-October and mid-December.

METEORITES

Sometimes great rocks fall to Earth from space. They are too big to burn away. We call them meteorites. Meteorites do not come from comets. Scientists think that asteroids sometimes crash and knock chunks off each other. These chunks eventually fall to Earth as meteorites.

Some meteorites are very large. The biggest found so far weighs over 60 tonnes and still lies where it fell hundreds of years ago in Africa. Meteorites made the craters on the Moon and other planets. Craters have also been made here on Earth. One of the best known is the Arizona Meteorite Crater in America. This huge crater is over a kilometre across and is nearly 200 metres deep. It was formed 20,000 years ago. Lots of other meteorite craters have been found, including a number in Australia. One of these, at Wolf Creek, is nearly a kilometre across.

Very large meteorites can cause a lot of damage when they land. If a meteorite the same size as those which caused the Arizona Meteorite or Wolf Creek craters hit London, there would be a large hole instead of a city. But don't worry – big meteorites are very rare!

Chapter 8
The Stars

Stars look like points of light in the sky. But they are really huge balls of hot gas. They shine like the Sun and seem faint only because they are so far away.

Stars are not like planets. Stars shine, while planets only reflect starlight. We see the other planets because the Sun lights them up. If the Sun suddenly went out, the planets would be plunged into darkness. They would seem to disappear.

THE LIFE OF A STAR

Stars are born inside huge clouds of gas and dust. We call these clouds nebulae. A famous example of a nebula in which stars are being born is the Orion Nebula (see page 77). As the new star gets smaller, it also becomes hotter, and starts to shine.

The Sun was born in this way. The Sun has been shining for about 5 billion years. It will continue to shine for another 5 billion years, until its fuel runs out. Then the Sun will swell to something about 100 times bigger than it is now. It will cool down and become red. After this it will shrink down into a very small, very heavy object, and will continue to shine feebly before it becomes cold and dead.

THE GREAT BEAR

The most famous pattern of stars in the sky is the Plough. This is only part of a much bigger pattern of fainter stars we call Ursa Major (the Great Bear). The seven stars making up the Plough form the bear's bottom and tail. In America, the pattern of stars we call the Plough is known as the Big Dipper. The pattern they form does look very much like a giant spoon.

The Plough is visible all year (if the sky is dark and clear). The North American

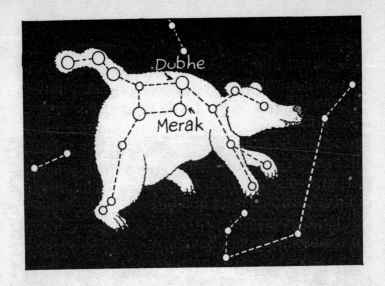

Indians thought that the three stars in the Plough "handle" were three hunters. They were chasing a bear around the sky. The bear was the four stars in the "bowl" of the Plough.

THE LITTLE BEAR

Once you have found the Plough, you can use it to show the way to the Pole-star. Follow a line from the star Merak through Dubhe as shown. You will soon come to the Pole-star. The Plough is in different parts of the sky at different times of the year. But its two end stars *always* point to the Pole-star.

The Pole-star is also called Polaris. It is the brightest star in the constellation Ursa Minor (the Little Bear). This is like a smaller, fainter copy of the Plough. Polaris lies at the end of the Little Bear's tail.

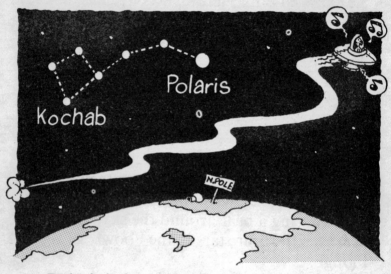

Polaris is at a point in the sky exactly above the Earth's North Pole. If you were standing at the North Pole, Polaris would be straight above you. When you are looking at Polaris, you are looking due north. If you look at the star Kochab through binoculars, you will notice its orangy-red colour.

There is a very old Greek legend about the two bears. This story is also about Jupiter, the King of the Gods. According to the story, Jupiter fell in love with the beautiful Callisto. This upset Jupiter's wife Juno! She was so angry that she turned Callisto into a bear. She also turned Callisto's son Arcas into a bear. Once Jupiter heard about this he changed both bears into constellations. He then placed them in the sky, where they can be seen to this day. Arcas is the Little Bear and Callisto the Great Bear.

You may have noticed that both bears have long tails. But bears on Earth have short tails. This is because when Jupiter threw Arcas and Callisto into the sky, he swung them round by their tails before letting go and their tails were stretched!

CASSIOPEIA

Now follow the line from the Plough to Polaris a bit further. You will then come to the pattern of stars we call Cassiopeia. This constellation is very easy to make out. Its main stars form a "W" or "M" (depending on which way up it is in the sky when you look at it). It is found on the opposite side of the Pole-star from the Plough.

If you have binoculars, look carefully for an orangy-yellow-coloured star. This is the star Schedir. A small telescope may show a faint blue star next to it. You will also be able so see another star, Achird, which is really a double star. It is formed from yellow and orange stars.

You will be able to see different stars at different times of the year. You can use the curved handle of the Plough as a pointer to other constellations.

In *spring*, if you follow the curve, you will come to Arcturus. This is the brightest star in the constellation Boötes (the Herdsman). The strong yellowy-orange colour of Arcturus can be easily seen with binoculars. The rest of Boötes looks like a huge kite in the sky.

Follow the line from the Plough handle

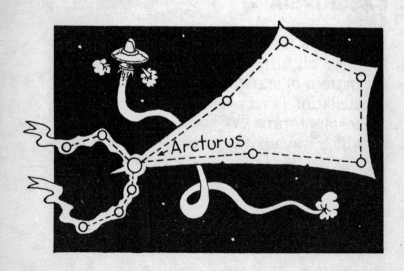

further and you will reach Spica. This is the brightest star in Virgo (the Virgin). Spica is white and is actually thousands of times brighter than the Sun. It seems much fainter because it is so far away. Virgo forms a Y-shaped pattern.

The three brightest stars in the *summer* night sky are Vega, Deneb and Altair. These stars are the first to appear as the sky becomes dark. They are known as the Summer Triangle.

Vega is the brightest star in the tiny constellation Lyra (the Lyre). It is also the brightest of the three stars in the Summer Triangle.

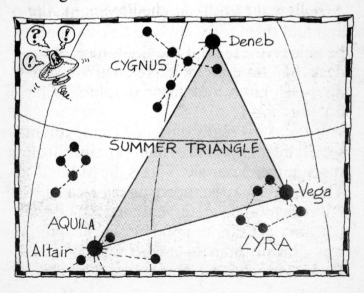

Deneb marks the tail of Cygnus (the Swan). It is the faintest of the three stars forming the Summer Triangle. Deneb, like Spica in the spring sky, is really thousands of times brighter than the Sun. It seems so faint only because it is a long way away.

The head of Cygnus is marked by Albireo. If you have a small telescope, you will see that Albireo is a double star. The two stars forming Albireo are yellow and blue.

The third member of the Summer Triangle is Altair. This is in the constellation Aquila (the Eagle).

Lying near the Summer Triangle are two small constellations. These are Sagitta (the Arrow) and Delphinus (the Dolphin). Try and find them for yourselves. You should be able to see them if the sky is nice and dark. Sagitta does look like an arrow. But does Delphinus look like a dolphin? What do you think?

If the sky is really dark and clear, you may see a faint misty band of light running through the Summer Triangle. This is the Milky Way. The Milky Way is known as the Heavenly River in an old Japanese legend which tells the story of Orihime and Hikoboshi. Orihime was a beautiful maiden who made material for kimono dresses. Her material had lovely

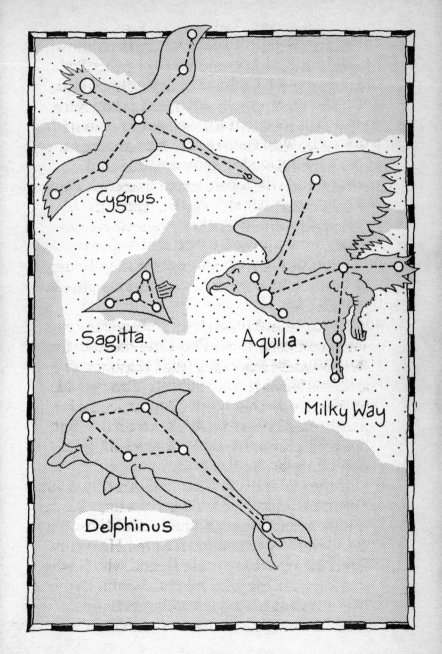

Cygnus.

Sagitta.

Aquila

Milky Way

Delphinus

73

colours and beautiful patterns and was known far and wide. Hikoboshi was a shepherd who fell in love with Orihime. They got married and went on a long honeymoon. They were so much in love that they began to stop their work to be with each other. This angered the gods, who decided to punish them, and Orihime and Hikoboshi were separated. They were put on either side of the Heavenly River and made to work.

They were allowed to see each other on one night of the year, but only if the sky was clear. This is on 7 July. If it rains on this night, the Heavenly River will flood and they will not meet. On 7 July, clear skies are prayed for so that Orihime and Hikoboshi can get together. It is a holiday for Japanese children, who pin messages on bamboo plants asking for presents.

If you want to see Orihime and Hikoboshi, look for the Summer Triangle. It is high in the south during summer evenings. The bottom star, Altair, is the shepherd Hikoboshi. Vega is his wife, Orihime. On clear, dark nights a faint misty band of light can be seen passing between them. This is the Heavenly River.

The two main *autumn* constellations are Andromeda and Pegasus. In Greek legend,

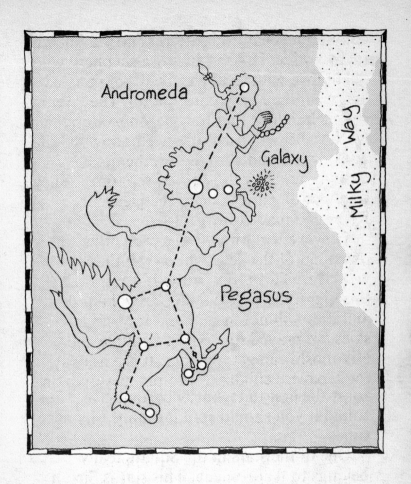

Andromeda was a beautiful princess and Pegasus was a famous winged horse.

The Square of Pegasus is made up of four stars. When seen on star charts, the Square seems brighter than it really is. In fact it doesn't stand out as well as you might think. You may have to look hard

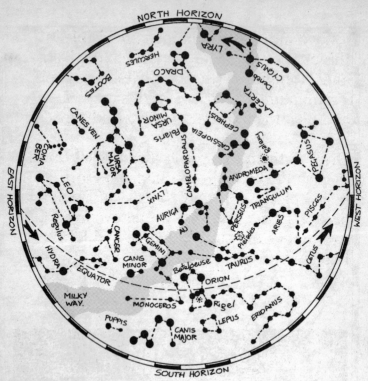

EAST HORIZON

WEST HORIZON

SOUTH HORIZON

for it the first time, but once you have found it you should spot it more easily next time.

One of the stars in the Square really belongs to Andromeda. This star is Sirrah. It has been "borrowed" only to make up the Square. The rest of Pegasus is much fainter. If the sky is dark and clear, try to pick out the other stars in Pegasus.

Andromeda is made up of a line of stars joined on to the corner of the Square of Pegasus.

Two more constellations are visible in this area of sky. They are Aries (the Ram) and Triangulum (the Triangle). Aries and Triangulum are shown on this map. Try and pick them out just below Andromeda.

Orion is the most splendid constellation in the *winter* sky. Its four main stars form a huge oblong. It is easy to pick out and can be seen in the south on winter evenings. Its two main stars are Betelgeuse and Rigel. Betelgeuse is a red supergiant star. Rigel is white. The two colours stand out against each other.

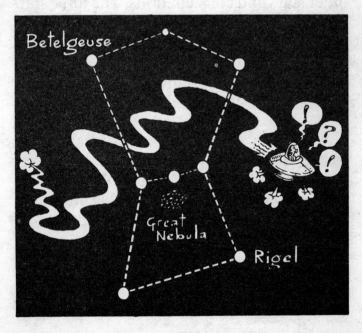

Look carefully just below the Belt of Orion. You should see a faint misty patch of light. This is the Orion Nebula. The Orion Nebula is a vast cloud of gas. It lies 1,500 light years away and is twenty light years across!

The Orion Nebula shows up well through binoculars. It is found in a line of faint stars marking the Sword of Orion. Look at the Belt and Sword of Orion through binoculars. Together they are a pretty sight. Stars are being born inside the Orion Nebula. These newly formed stars are very hot. They are making the gas in the Orion Nebula shine.

Orion can be used as a pointer to many other stars and constellations. The three stars in the middle of Orion are known as Orion's Belt. They point the way to the bright star Sirius. This is the brightest star in the whole sky (apart from the Sun!) It is part of the constellation Canis Major (the Great Dog).

MAKING A STAR-CLOCK

For centuries, we have been able to tell the time during the day by using a sundial. As we have seen, a simple shadow-clock consists of a flat dial marked off in hours (rather like a clock face), together with an upright stick. As the day progresses and the

Sun appears to move around the sky, the position of the shadow of the stick on the sundial also changes. It falls across the dial, showing the time.

But what about night-time, when there isn't any Sun? Why not make a simple star-clock? It is easy to make and fun to use when the sky is clear.

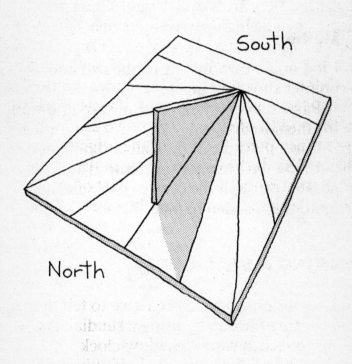

What You Will Need to Make the Star-clock

- A sheet of paper
- A sheet of card
- Paper paste
- Scissors
- A piece of wood approximately 200 mm long × 25 mm wide × 5 mm thick
- A drawing-pin

Method

First of all, carefully draw the dial and pointer shown opposite.

Paste them on to a piece of card and wait for them to dry.

Carefully cut out the dial and pointer.

Using the drawing-pin, fasten the pointer through the centre of the dial and on to the wooden handle.

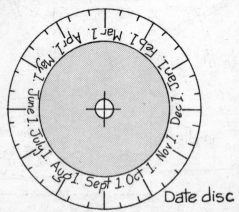

Date disc

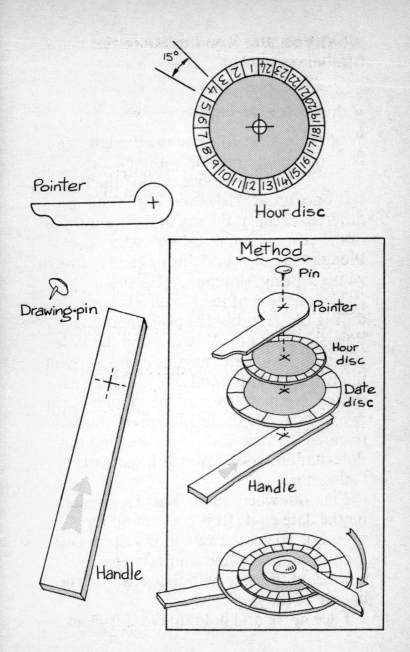

15°

Pointer

Hour disc

Drawing-pin

Handle

Method

Pin

Pointer

Hour
disc

Date
disc

Handle

Handle

Draw an arrow on the handle just below the dial, as shown.

Using the Star-clock

We use the stars forming the Plough (see page 67) to tell the time with our star-clock. The Plough moves round the Pole-star once a day. However, it is found in different areas of the sky at different times of the year. This chart shows where the Plough may be found during the evening in winter, spring, summer and autumn.

The position of the Plough changes during the year, but the position of the Pole-star does not. You can find the Pole-star by drawing an imaginary line through the two stars at the end of the Plough as shown. No matter where the Plough is, the two stars at end of the Plough *always* point towards the Pole-star. Once you find the Pole-star and look towards it, you are facing north.

Find out where today's date is situated on the date circle (this runs round the outside). The date circle shows the twelve months and each line counts as ten days.

Line up the date with the arrow on the handle of the star-clock.

Face north and hold up the star-clock,

lining up the drawing-pin as closely
as possible with the Pole-star. This might
be a little difficult because the star-clock
covers up the Pole-star, but do the best
you can!

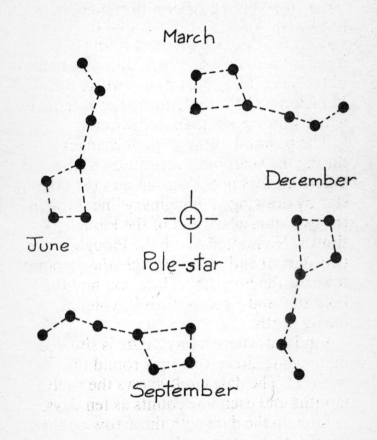

March

December

June

Pole-star

September

North Horizon

Hold the dial and the handle firmly together by pressing down with your thumb.

Put the edge of the pointer in line with the two stars at the end of the Plough.

Read off the time. This is given as a twenty-four-hour clock on the inner circle of the dial.

Chapter 9

Some Tips for Star-gazers

Choose a clear night. It's no good looking for stars if the sky is hidden by clouds! And the darker the sky, the more easily you will be able to see the stars and planets. If you can, get away from street lights. But *never* go away from home on your own. Go with an adult or a group of friends. Even moonlight can make it difficult to see faint objects, so try to pick a night when the Moon isn't in the sky. Unless, of course, you want to look at the Moon itself!

Make sure you wrap up warmly. You will be standing fairly still for a long time, and it's surprising how cold you can get, even during summer evenings. Most of the heat from your body is lost through your head, so it's important to wear a hat. You'll need gloves, too, and the sort with cut-off fingers are a good idea, so that you can hold any equipment and write things down. Finally, don't forget your feet. Be careful not to wear tight shoes, which will make your toes feel very cold quite quickly.

Looking up at the sky can give you a stiff neck, so another idea is to wrap yourself up in a sleeping-bag and lie out on a sun-lounger. But don't get too comfortable or you may fall asleep!

When you first go outside, give your eyes time to get used to the dark. This may take at least ten minutes. Once you've got your "night vision", don't spoil it by using a bright light to find your way around. The best thing is to use a red light. Don't worry if you haven't got a red torch. You can always put a piece of transparent red plastic (maybe a sweet wrapper) over the end of your torch.

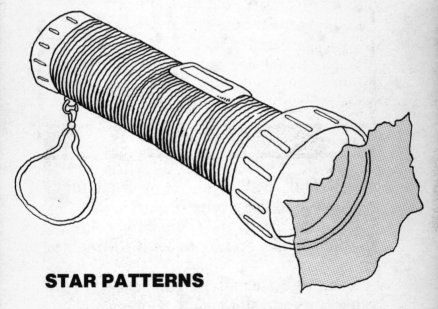

STAR PATTERNS

So, now that you are dressed up warmly and your eyes are used to the dark, you are ready to start star-gazing. But what do you look at first? You should begin by learning a few star patterns. Some are quite

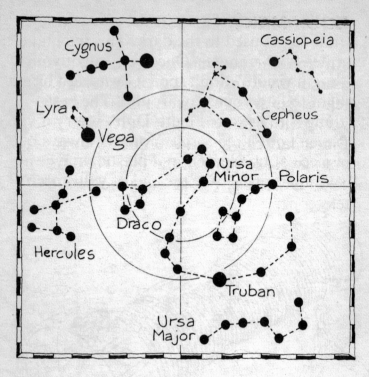

easy to find: the Plough (see page 67), for example, and the groups of stars Cassiopeia, Orion and Canis Major. Look for their shapes and try to see their brightest stars.

Some of these patterns can be used to find other stars and star groups. For example, the diagram on page 83 shows you how to find Polaris (the Pole-star) by using two stars in the Plough as pointers. Spend a few nights just looking and learning and you will soon start to find your way around.

EQUIPMENT

Anyone who becomes interested in astronomy wants to own a telescope. But telescopes are expensive. It is far better to get a pair of binoculars to start with. Binoculars can be used for lots of things, not just for looking at the sky. They are also much easier to carry around than a telescope.

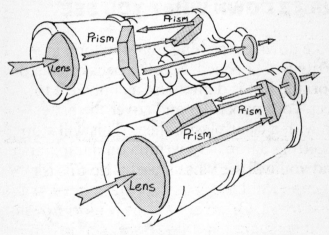

Binoculars are really two small telescopes held together. They are easy to handle and use. When you look through binoculars, you use both eyes at the same time. This is more comfortable than closing one eye as when using a telescope.

If you *are* thinking of buying a pair of binoculars or a telescope, make sure you ask for plenty of advice first. They are very expensive, so it's important to get the ones which are going to be most useful to you.

But to begin with there's plenty for you to see without using binoculars or a telescope. As you learn what to look for, you'll be surprised just how many things you can find and watch in space.

WRITE DOWN WHAT YOU SEE

Note down everything that you look at. Write with a pencil, because pens often stop working if it is damp! Use a clipboard to keep your paper flat and cover the paper up with a clear plastic sheet. This will stop it getting damp. Try writing on damp paper and you will see what a useful tip this is!

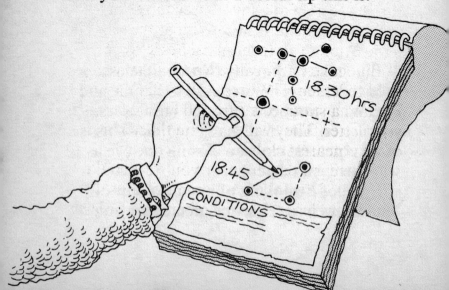

Why not make yourself a log-book?
You could then record everything you
see. Use an exercise book with blank and
ruled pages. You can draw what you see on
the blank pages and make notes on the
others.

Each time you write something down,
include the time and date and say if you
were using binoculars or a telescope.
Mention where you were, and what the sky
was like (e.g. clear or cloudy).

TAKING IT FURTHER

Astronomy is a lot of fun, even on your
own. But it is even better when you star-
gaze with fellow astronomers! Why not join
a local astronomy club? Your local library
should be able to tell you how to get in
touch with them. If not, write to the
Federation of Astronomical Societies, c/o
"Whitehaven", Maytree Road, Lower
Moor, Pershore, Worcs. WR10 2NY.
Enclose a stamped addressed envelope with
your letter. They will give you the address
of your nearest club.

If there isn't a club near you, you could
join one of the following organizations.
They all welcome new members and publish

regular magazines and newsletters. Please remember, if you do get in touch with any of them, mention your age.

Junior Astronomical Society,
    36 Fairway,
    Keyworth,
    Nottingham NG12 5DU,
    England

Astronomical Society of the Pacific,
    390 Ashton Avenue,
    San Francisco
    CA 94112,
    USA

Royal Astronomical Society of Canada,
    McLaughlin Planetarium,
    100 Queens Park,
    Toronto,
    Ontario,
    Canada M5S 2C6

Index